Animal Neighbours
Rat

Stephen Savage

HODDER
Wayland

An imprint of Hodder Children's Books

Animal Neighbours

Titles in this series:

Badger • Bat • Deer • Fox • Hare • Hedgehog Mole • Mouse • Otter • Owl • Rat • Swallow

Conceived and produced for Hodder Wayland by

Nutshell
MEDIA

Intergen House, 65–67 Western Road, Hove BN3 2JQ, UK
www.nutshellmedialtd.co.uk

Commissioning Editor: Vicky Brooker
Designer: Tim Mayer
Illustrator: Jackie Harland
Picture Research: Glass Onion Pictures

Published in Great Britain in 2004 by Hodder Wayland, an imprint of Hodder Children's Books.

British Library Cataloguing in Publication Data
Savage, Stephen, 1965–
Rat. – (Animal neighbours)
1. Rats – Juvenile literature
I. Title
599.3'52

ISBN 0 7502 4479 8

Cover: A brown rat at the end of a sewer pipe.
Title page: A brown rat in a derelict building.

Picture acknowledgements
FLPA 11 (R. Bird), 19 (Terry Whittaker), 20 (R. P. Lawrence), 21 (Terry Whittaker); naturepl.com *Title page*
(Paul Hobson), 10 (David Tipling), 12 (Warwick Sloss), 24 (David Kjaer), 2 bottom (David Tipling);
NHPA *Cover* (Stephen Dalton), 8 (Daniel Heuclin), 13, 25 (Stephen Dalton), 28 top (Daniel Heuclin);
Oxford Scientific Films 6 (John Downer), 7 (Paul Berquist/AA), 9 (Robin Redfern), 14 (Irvine Cushing),
15 (Mark Hamblin), 16–17 (John Downer), 22 (Robin Redfern), 23 (Tony Tilford), 26 (Michael Leach),
27 (Ian West), 28 right (Robin Redfern), 28 left (Tony Tilford).

Colour reproductions by Dot Gradations Ltd, UK
Printed and bound in China.

Hodder Children's Books
A division of Hodder Headline Limited
338 Euston Road, London NW1 3BH

Contents

Meet the Rat

Rats are agile, intelligent rodents. They have adapted to almost every habitat, from fields and forests, to deserts, towns and cities. Rats are found almost everywhere in the world apart from the polar regions.

This book looks at the brown rat, one of the most widespread of all the rat species.

Ears

Rats have an excellent sense of hearing, which is their main sense for detecting danger. They can also hear the communication sounds made by other rats.

Eyes

Rats can see well up to about a metre away, but over longer distances their eyes can only sense movement.

Nose

Rats have an acute sense of smell, which is used for finding food. It is also used to detect scents that mark territory, or to recognise other rats.

Teeth

Like all rodents, rats have sharp incisor teeth, which continue to grow throughout their lives. The teeth must be ground down by gnawing on hard objects to stop them growing too long. Molars further back in the cheek grind up food before it is swallowed.

Whiskers

Whiskers are very sensitive to touch. They help the rat to find its way around in the dark.

Fore feet

The fore feet are smaller than the hind feet. They can be used when running or walking, or to hold food while eating.

Fur

Rats have long, oily, waterproof fur, which helps protect them against the cold and the damp.

RAT FACTS

The brown rat's scientific name is *Rattus novegicus*, from the Latin words *novegicus* meaning 'Norwegian' and *rattus* meaning 'rat'.

Other common names include Norwegian rat, wharf rat, common rat, water rat, sewer rat and house rat.

Male rats are known as bucks, females as does and young rats as pups. A group of rats is known as a mischief.

The brown rat's body measures about 28 cm long without the tail. The tail is almost as long as the body. Adult brown rats weigh between 200 and 400 g.

Tail

A rat's tail is long, scaly and almost completely hairless. It is held up in the air for balance while walking along narrow objects or when swimming.

◀ A brown rat.

Hind legs

The rat's hind legs are long and powerful. The hind feet are large for running and climbing. Each toe ends with a tiny claw.

▲ This shows the size of a rat compared to an adult human hand.

The Rat Family

Rats belong to the largest group of mammals, a group that scientists call the 'mouse-like group of rodents'. This group includes various species of rats, mice, voles and hamsters. Members of the group are all mouse-shaped, but they can vary greatly in size. Many dig burrows, where they live in colonies.

▼ **This black rat in India is stealing some tea from a glass.**

BLACK DEATH

In medieval times, the black rat was responsible for spreading the bubonic plague (also called the black death). This disease killed thousands of people in Europe. Fleas infected with the plague bacteria passed the disease to rats through bites. The disease passed to other fleas that bit the infected rat. People bitten by an infected flea or a rat caught the disease.

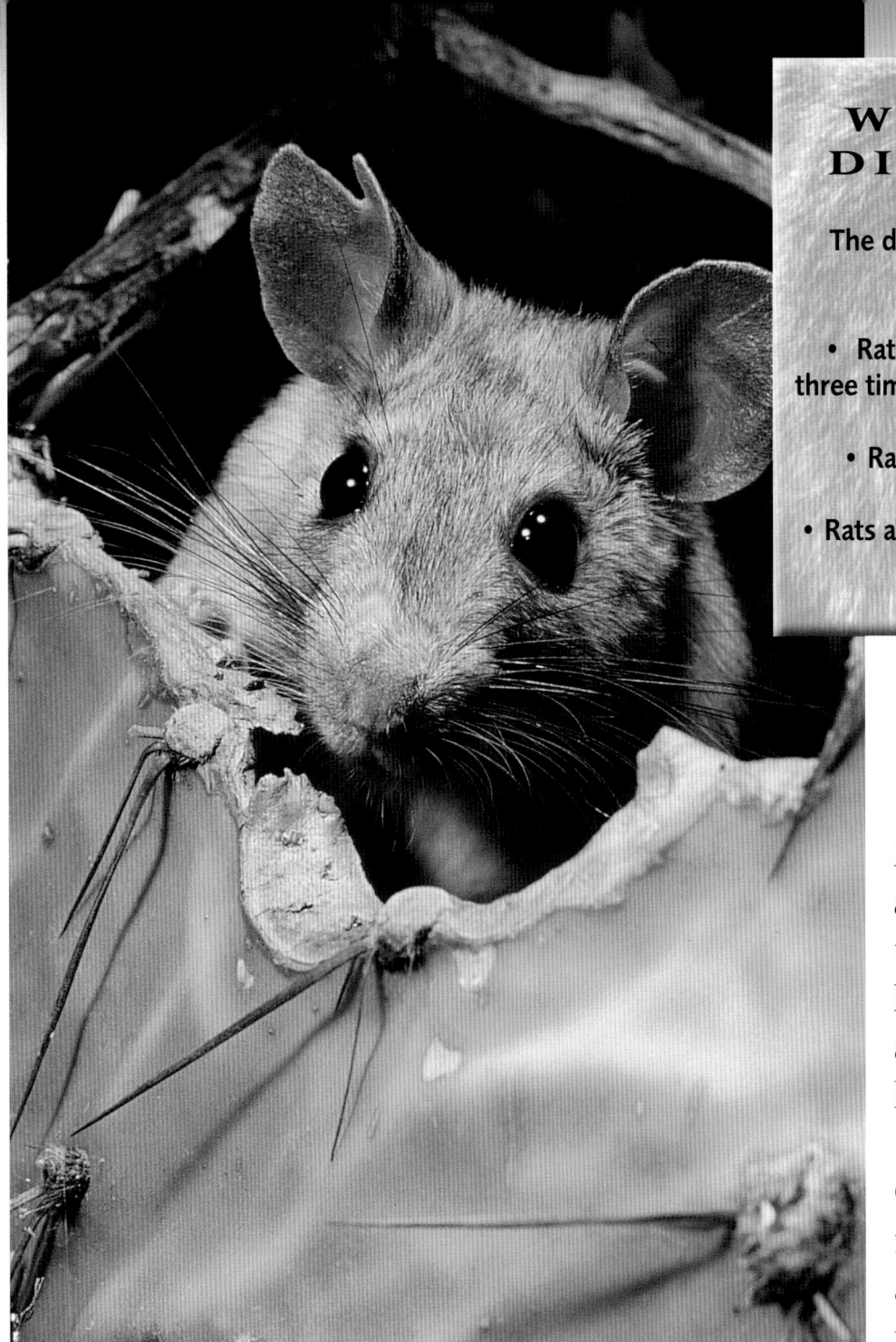

WHAT'S THE DIFFERENCE?

The differences between a rat and a mouse are:

• Rats are bigger. The brown rat is three times as long as the house mouse.

• Rats have longer, thicker tails.

• Rats are good swimmers. Mice prefer not to swim.

Many rat species, such as the brown rat and the black rat, live near humans, often in or around homes, or near human activity.

Other types of rat live far away from humans and some are quite rare. The Australian stick-nest rat can only be found on a small island off the coast of Australia. It makes a strong nest from sticks up to 1.5 metres high. The desert pack rat lives in the deserts of North and Central America. It feeds on seeds, cactus and other plants. Cactus plants are also a good source of water in this rat's desert habitat.

▲ Desert pack rats often build their nests in cacti. Apart from food, the cacti provide shelter from extreme desert temperatures and protection from predators.

Birth and Growing Up

Rats can be born at any time of year, although most are born in the spring or autumn. Before she gives birth, a pregnant doe makes a loose, round nest from dried grass and straw. She builds it in a chamber underground, where she will be safe from the prying eyes of predators.

The new-born rat pups are pink, blind and deaf, born with their eyes and ears tightly closed and with no fur. When they are about 3 days old the pups may start to crawl, but they cannot move far.

RAT PUPS

New-born pups are about 4 cm long and weigh between 5–7 g.

The average sized litter is seven pups, although larger does can give birth to as many as thirteen.

▼ A litter of six new-born pups huddle together in the nest for warmth.

▲ These 18-day-old pups jostle with each other as they drink their mother's milk.

The rat pups rely on their mother for food and protection. She cleans and suckles them several times a day and only leaves the nest to find food for herself. If the pups become distressed or cold, they make a high-pitched call to their mother.

Rat pups grow rapidly. By the time they are a week old, they are covered in a soft coat of fur and their eyes are open. Their teeth begin to grow when they are about 10 days old and they are able to hear from about 12 days. The pups can now walk and begin to explore the nest chamber.

▲ These two young rats are exploring their surroundings.

Early days

At 2 weeks old, the pups begin to leave the nest, following their mother as she looks for food. This is the time they get their first taste of solid food, copying their mother as she nibbles at seeds or waste food. Even though they have started to eat solid food, the doe continues to suckle her pups back at the nest.

Over the next week the pups follow their mother on her foraging trips, learning the pathways that lead to food, escape routes, and dangerous areas to avoid in the area surrounding the nest.

At about 3 weeks old, the pups are completely weaned and eat just solid food. By now they may weigh more than 80 grams. They grow so quickly that their bodies do not grow in proportion. Young rats have large heads and feet compared with the rest of their body.

By the time they are 3 months old, the young rats have their adult fur and are fully grown. They may remain with the adult group, or travel to a new, unoccupied area.

▼ Young rats can often be seen foraging on rubbish tips, where food is easy to find.

Habitat

Rats can survive in many types of habitat, as long as they can find food, water and shelter. Many live near people, taking advantage of their food and buildings. Rats are common in towns and large cities, where they are attracted by food waste.

Many rats live in or around houses, in warehouses and around docks. Others live on rubbish tips and wasteland. Some rats are attracted to gardens where people put out food for wild birds, or to places where pets are kept, tempted by their food and their bedding. Rats also live underground in sewer pipes, where they nest and find food.

▲ Rats are very agile rodents, with powerful hind legs for leaping and climbing.

SWIMMING

Rats are excellent swimmers and can hold their breath under water for four minutes. They can tread water and stay afloat for up to three days. Brown rats are able to swim against the water flow in sewage pipes, allowing them to move up and down the sewage system. They can even scamper through plumbing pipes and come up through toilets in disused houses.

In the countryside, rats live in barns, grain stores or places where farm animals are kept. They often live near water, especially on riverbanks and around ponds. Since they are good swimmers, water provides an escape route from predators, as well as a source of food and drink.

▼ Rats exit sewage systems at different places to find new sources of food.

The burrow

When not living in buildings or other artificial structures, rats live underground. They live in a burrow, a tunnel system that they dig themselves. Rats use their front feet for digging soil, which they push under their body and out behind them with their hind feet.

The burrow is made up of several tunnels connected together, and one or more chambers for nesting, resting or feeding. When a tunnel system is first dug, it is only 30–50 centimetres in length. However, as a rat colony grows, more tunnels are added.

▲ A brown rat checks for signs of danger before leaving the safety of its burrow.

▼ Rats that make their burrow near rivers and ponds have a constant supply of drinking water.

Each burrow has one main entrance and many exits for a quick escape in times of danger. The entrance is usually dug in places where there is dense vegetation to hide beneath. This is often on sloping ground, such as a ditch or a riverbank. In a garden, the entrance may be against the wall of a house, on a rockery, or beneath a garden shed.

Territory and packs

Rats live in colonies, called packs. A large pack can be made up of smaller groups, called clans. Each clan or pack has a dominant male, and a group of does known as its harem. The dominant male is usually the biggest buck. He will mate with the largest does, which he accepts into his harem.

Each pack lives within its own territory, which is usually between 15–45 metres around the central burrow. Rats mark the borders of their territory with urine, and with scent

MIGRATIONS

When there are too many rats living in one area, they sometimes carry out mass migrations. They swarm out into the streets looking for a new place to live with fewer rats. The German name for the brown rat is *wanderratte*, which means 'roving rat', after these migrations.

▲ These rats have spilt out on to the streets in search of a new, less crowded place to live.

produced from special glands on the sides of their bodies. This is called scent-marking.

Rats have a group scent and can recognise other members of the pack through their smell. The bucks in each pack defend the territory from intruders, and fights can break out over territory borders or food.

Where there is plenty of food and shelter, territories are smaller because the rats do not need to travel far to get what they need. Large packs containing hundreds of rats can often be found around refuse tips and sewers, where there is enough food and shelter to support many rats. In areas where food is scarce, territories are larger.

Food

Rats are omnivores, which means they eat both plants and animals. Their favourite food is grain. Rural rats feed on cereal crops, or cereal grain in grain stores. Urban rats feed on biscuits, bread and other foods made from grain, but they will also eat almost anything that humans eat. They are particularly attracted by food waste.

▼ Brown rats are at the centre of several food chains. (The illustrations are not to scale.)

Rat food chain

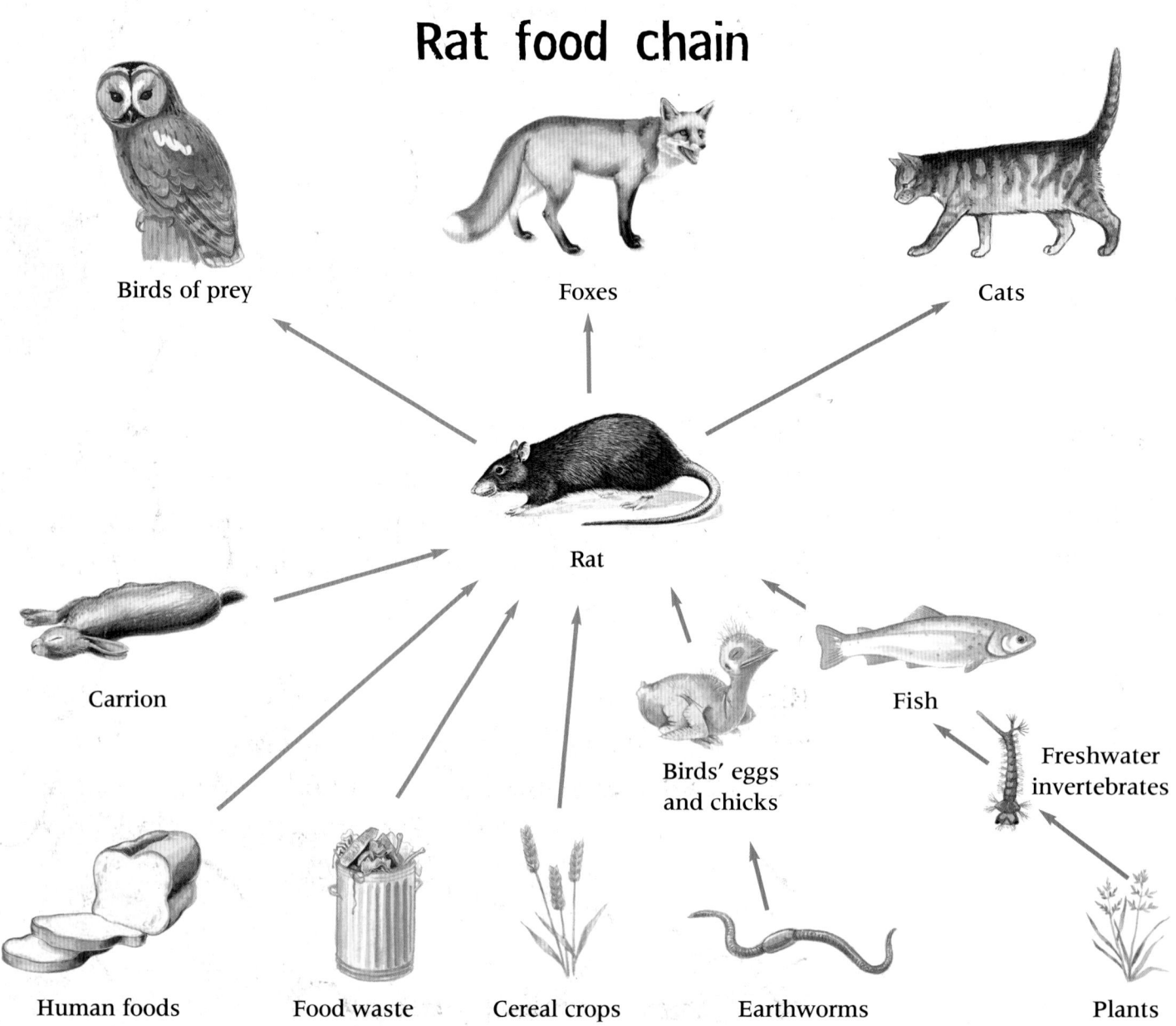

Birds of prey

Foxes

Cats

Rat

Carrion

Birds' eggs and chicks

Fish

Freshwater invertebrates

Human foods

Food waste

Cereal crops

Earthworms

Plants

▲ A hen will risk her own life to protect her eggs from predators such as rats.

Rats living near water catch fish and other small, aquatic creatures. They will also scavenge, eating the remains of dead animals, called carrion. Rats living near the coast feed on dead animals that are washed up on the shore at high tide.

Bird chicks and their eggs are another favourite food, especially those of ground-nesting birds such as waterfowl and swans. The rat will usually try to steal the chicks or eggs from the nest while the parents are away, but sometimes they take them when the parents are present. Rats can kill chickens if they are cornered and cannot escape, and they occasionally kill and eat small mammals such as mice.

Foraging

Since most of the rat's activity takes place at night, it relies on its sense of touch, using special body hairs and whiskers to find its way around in the dark. It also uses its excellent sense of smell to find food and avoid danger. Rats are particularly wary of any new scents they encounter. If a rat finds food out in the open, it will carry the food in its mouth to a safer place before eating.

Drinking water is very important for rats. In the countryside, they drink from ponds, streams and puddles. Rats living in sewers beneath cities have a constant supply of water. In gardens, they can drink from ponds and bird baths. Inside a house, they reach water from toilets and sinks. They even lick the water that has condensed on pipes.

▲ Hanging upside-down, this rat is trying to get at the nuts in this bird feeder.

▲ On farms, rats often eat grain meant for livestock, such as this hen feed.

Runs

Rats are very intelligent and memorise the various routes, or runs, in their territory. When looking for food, the rat searches randomly at first. But once it has found a source of food, the rat will remember the shortest route to it and use the run again and again.

Finding a Mate

When they reach a weight of about 115 grams, does are able to mate. This is usually after they are 11 weeks old. Young bucks are not able to mate until they are older, because they grow slower in the company of a dominant male. This reduces the amount of breeding bucks in a pack at one time, which means there is less fighting.

▼ You can tell the difference between a doe and a buck because the buck (on the right below) is usually bigger.

BREEDING

Rats breed throughout most of the year.

The pups are born between 21 and 23 days after mating.

The average doe has four to seven litters of pups a year, successfully weaning 20 pups or more.

After the birth of her pups, the doe is able to mate again 18 hours later.

▶ This buck is finding out whether the doe is ready to mate.

Adult does are ready to mate every four or five days for about 20 hours. They will only mate with the dominant male in the pack. When a doe is ready, she gives the buck a signal by producing a special chemical from her body, called a pheromone. There is no courtship between the buck and the doe and the buck leaves the doe to make a nest and rear her pups on her own.

23

Threats

Rats, especially young rats, have many predators. In the countryside, mammals such as weasels and foxes prey on rats. Birds of prey such as hawks and owls are also major predators. In towns and cities, cats and dogs prey on rats.

Younger rats can be prevented from reaching food at night by older and larger rats in the pack. They live on the edges of a pack and can be forced to look for food during the day, when they are an easy target for predators.

When food is scarce, rats can go without food for about two weeks. However, in such situations, rats may resort to cannibalism, eating the younger and weaker members of the pack. Does will fiercely defend their nest and young from attack by other rats.

▶ **The nocturnal European wild cat hunts mainly rabbits and rodents, including rats.**

LIFESPAN

Rats can live for up to 3 years in the wild, but few live beyond the age of 2 and most survive for only a year. Despite their short lifespan, rats produce so many litters of young a year that rat populations in an area remain the same or may even increase.

▼ Rats have excellent hearing to detect predators, but barn owls swoop down on their prey in silence and take them by surprise.

People and rats

The brown rat's biggest threat is people. Rats have been killed as pests for thousands of years, but they still exist today in increasingly large numbers. On farms they damage crops and stored grain. In buildings they do a lot of damage gnawing wood, electricity cables, and even concrete and metal. Rats not only eat our foods, they contaminate it by nibbling or leaving droppings, making it unfit to eat.

CONTAMINATION

Rats contaminate three times the amount of food that they eat. They destroy more than US$250 million of the world's stored and growing food each year, which would be enough to feed 200 million people.

▼ Rats eat and damage stored food. This rat has got into a box of potatoes.

The biggest reason why people kill rats is because they carry diseases that humans can catch. They can infect people's food with bacteria that causes food poisoning, which can make people very ill. They can also transmit Weil's disease through their urine. This bacteria can live in damp places and infect humans and domestic animals through cuts and grazes.

▶ Pet rats are slower and more docile than their wild relatives. If properly looked after, they do not pass diseases to their owners.

PET RATS

Rats have been specially bred as pets from wild brown rats, possibly since the mid-1800s. It is thought that this was done by breeding albino (white) rats with brown ones. Over many generations, this created a variety of colours including fawn, champagne, and lilac.

Rat Life Cycle

1 New-born rat pups are blind, deaf and furless. An average litter will have between six and eleven pups.

5 Does are ready to mate when they are about 11 weeks old. Bucks develop more slowly when a dominant male is present.

2 At 1 week old the pups are covered in soft fur and their eyes are open. They can hear when they are 12 days old.

4 At about 3 weeks old the pups are completely weaned and eat only solid food. Their mother may be pregnant again.

3 At about 2 weeks old, the pups follow their mother on feeding trips and start to eat solid food.

Rat Clues

Look out for the following clues to help you find signs of a rat:

Burrow entrance
The entrance to a rat's burrow is usually a hole between 70–120 mm in diameter, made in grassy banks, under tree roots, or at the edge of paving or drain cover surrounds.

Nest
A loose ball of plant material, paper, cloth or other materials may be a sign that rats are nesting nearby. Nests can be found in lofts or under floorboards.

Runs
Rats follow the same routes, or runs, through their territory every night. Outside they may leave trails through grass and low vegetation. The trails look like walkways beneath the vegetation.

Gnawing marks
Look for signs of gnawing on non-food materials. Teeth marks are small and usually appear lighter than the rest of the wood.

Droppings
Rat droppings are found along trails frequently used by rats. They are small, black and cylindrical, and slightly tapered at both ends.

12 mm

Grease marks
Rats often leave rub marks against walls, pipes or holes in buildings. These are greasy deposits left by the oils in the rats' fur.

Sounds
Rats make occasional squeaks or scuttling sounds as they run about behind a wall or in a loft. The most common sound of a rat is its gnawing.

Footprints
Rats have four toes on the fore foot and five toes on the hind foot. Prints may be seen in the dust in buildings or in the mud by a stream or pond.

Hind foot   Front foot

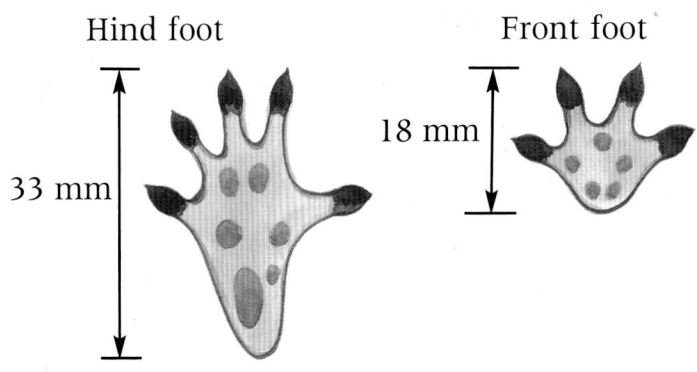

33 mm   18 mm

Glossary

aquatic Living in water, for example an animal that can live all or part of the time in water.

bacteria Microscopic creatures that live all around us. Some are useful, while others cause disease.

buck A male rat. The males of other species, such as deer, rabbits and squirrels are also called bucks.

carrion The body of a dead animal that is found and eaten by another animal.

cereal crops Crops such as wheat, barley and maize, which produce grain that is used for food.

colony A group of the same type of animals that live together.

contaminate To make something impure by having contact with it.

doe A female rat. The females of other animal species such as deer, rabbits and squirrels are also called does.

dominant The largest, strongest animal of the group.

foraging Searching for food.

habitat The area where an animal or plant naturally lives.

incisor teeth Sharp teeth at the front of the mouth used for biting or cutting.

litter A group of young animals born at the same time.

molars Blunt teeth at the back of the mouth used for chewing or grinding food.

omnivore An animal that eats both plants and animals.

pack A group of rats that live together. Wolves also live in a pack.

predator An animal that hunts and eats other animals.

prey Animals that are killed and eaten by predators.

pup A young rat. Young dogs, seals and bats are also called pups.

rodents A group of mammals that have two incisor teeth in each jaw for gnawing. Mice, rats, squirrels, porcupines and beavers are rodents.

rural A habitat in the countryside.

scavenge To eat the dead remains of other animals.

suckle To feed young from teats.

territory The area that is defended and controlled by an animal.

urban A habitat in a town or city.

vegetation Various different plants that grow together forming a covering on the ground.

weaned Used to eating solid food rather than a mother's milk.

Finding Out More

Other books to read

Animal Young: Mammals by Rod Theodorou (Heinemann, 1999)

Classification: Animal Kingdom by Kate Whyman (Hodder Wayland, 2000)

Classifying Living Things: Classifying Mammals by Andrew Solway (Heinemann, 2003)

Illustrated Encyclopedia of Animals by Fran Pickering (Chrysalis, 2003)

Life Cycles: Cats and Other Mammals by Sally Morgan (Chrysalis, 2001)

Living Nature: Mammals by Angela Royston (Chrysalis, 2002)

My Pet: Rats and Mice by Honor Head (Chrysalis, 2001)

The Wayland Book of Common British Mammals by Shirley Thompson (Hodder Wayland, 2000)

Weird Wildlife: Mammals by Jen Green (Chrysalis, 2002)

What's the Difference?: Mammals by Stephen Savage (Hodder Wayland, 2002)

Wild Britain: Towns & Cities by R. & L. Spilsbury (Heinemann, 2003)

Organisations to contact

Countryside Foundation for Education
PO Box 8, Hebden Bridge HX7 5YJ
www.countrysidefoundation.org.uk
An organisation that produces training and teaching materials to help the understanding of the countryside and its problems.

English Nature
Northminster House, Peterborough, Cambridgeshire PE1 1UA
www.englishnature.org.uk
A government body that promotes the conservation of English wildlife and the natural environment.

The Mammal Society
2B Inworth Street, London SW11 3EP
www.abdn.ac.uk/mammal/newsite/
This organisation promotes the study and conservation of British mammals.

Wildlife Watch
National Office, The Kiln, Waterside, Mather Road, Newark NG24 1WT
www.wildlifetrusts.org
The junior branch of the Wildlife Trusts, a network of local Wildlife Trusts caring for nearly 2,500 nature reserves, from rugged coastline to urban wildlife havens, protecting a huge number of habitats and species.

Index

Page numbers in **bold** refer to a photograph or illustration.